Epic Philosophies in Love, War, & Reasoning
Vol. 1:

Twisted Men with Twisted Minds

By
Thomas S. Doland

Dedicated to my mother, Ida.

TABLE OF CONTENTS

Preface

Traveling the world's nations and cultures breaks the mold of encapsulated thinking. It opens human suffering and passion. Societies torn by culture wars worldwide. Reveal the tenderness of the human drama. From towers of power dynasties to hidden slave camps, the orphans of compassion seek asylum.

Mysteries of culture hidden by colorful tradition hide the trauma of caste systems. Heartless governments uprooting families into endless migration to nowhere. Highways of broken dreams and lives seeking hope for new life and fulfillment. These works capture the essence of the ocean's tides and waves of love, desire, passion, and vision.

Let your imagination relocate you to another world. Perhaps the refueling of your own existence.
Welcome to the travels into your heart and soul.

Introduction

The human experience is not without constant assault from many different sources. This volume takes eye-opening realities from surprising experiences. The realistic approaches give the reader an actual journey into the events in a very visual word experience, questions, answers, doubts, wrapped in the success and failure of the menagerie of tales and sagas. You will experience your own deep emotions as you ride these waves of narration with twisted men with twisted minds.

Eyes Wide Open

Collaborating with himself
Man misleads his way
He has no guide inside him
Misunderstanding his whims

Religion claims understanding
More confusion in man's stay
Trusting in politicians play
Manipulating lies
Eyes open wide
Blind leads the blind

Where are the seers
They are hiding away
Collaborating with themselves
They mislead the way
They have no light inside them
Misunderstanding their stay

One religion annihilates
Another plays the fool
How can you know God
Allowing every lie to rule
Have you no eyes to see
No heart to understand
Man has lost his way
There is no one that can stand
To reveal the hidden majesty
His creation
Clear as a cloudless day

All Dressed Up

We embellish ourselves
With thoughts untamed
Through unknown paths
With unknown names
We think ourselves worthy
Of the greatest claims
Money can buy
our prideful fame

Its all in your mind
It's not reality
It's plain to see

You're still the same person
Dressed up in your head
Dressed up real fancy you see

You are still nothing more
Than when you began
Death waits for you
As he does for the poor

Its all in your mind
Its clear on the last page

Blowing In the Wind

Lightning flashed in the distance
Across the sky
Thunder roared
Shaking me inside

Scent of rain
Blowing in the wind
First drops are falling
It's about to begin

Dark clouds are forming
From a thousand years
Signs of man's torment
Proof of our fears

Have idealized your life and thoughts
Can you smell history's musty scent
The scent of conforming
To history's proven disasters

Lightning flashing across the sky
Roaring thunder I realize
We've learned nothing
To intellectualize

The children run
And don't know why
First drops from the sky

Anyone's Fool

From the dark side of life
The valiant ones rage
Filled with hate
Plans to do carnage
Bringing tools of their trade

Into the night
Their plans are made
Terrorize the innocent
Leave them bleeding and dazed
With stealth and darkness
They make a descent

The innocent live in their adorned cocoon
Living to themselves
Anyone's fool
They live for the money
They blow away

Jealousy hate and rage fill their eyes
Valiant ones waiting in darkness
Right victims they spy
Falling on prey like jungle cats
Thinking nothing of killing
American culture has seen to that

City Scape

Look from the tower on the city scape
Tell me what you see
Neon lights and buildings aglow
Traffic fills the streets
Hustle and bustle of the crowd
Gunfire breaks out
In the street below
The crowd clears away
Bodies lay in the street
Crying and shouting
fill the air
Melanda's gang made things equal again
Mother's cry and groan
Their son on the ground
Careless thoughts of payback aroused
Across the street
Church bells toll
For what are they ringing
Do you suppose
For you for me for nothing
Don't you see
This is America
Land of the free

Casual Glance

Feet shuffle restlessly
along the busy street
Life hustles along just rushing ahead
To find meaning in defeat
Left alone on a corner
What's relative and who's to care
Pain finds solace with pain
Something in common to share

There is triumph in anger
Prison released within
Loneliness given meaning
No father to call them in
Home is a dark place
Everyone hides true feelings
Crying silently in a crowded room
Bringing terror to their own blood
All find a common bond
Fighting to protect what's meaningless
Satisfaction borne in vengeance

Fears rage on
Fed by dread to survive
An end to insanity must come
Police can't heal a broken heart
You give a casual glance
Of indifference
Pistols and knives bring comfort

The war inside deeply instilled
If only a mother or father cared
Now its kill or be killed

A life wrestled to the ground
By the power of neglect
A city succumb to the numbness
within
The system blind
The money comes
Another committee of lies
Secures the fate
Who can penetrate
A defended city
Who can rescue
A broken soul
Who cares if they live
Who cares if they die
Only the ones
Whose life is on the cross

Day in the Life

Browsing through the morning paper
Coffee tastes really smooth
Reminded me of my mother
Making coffee milk and waffles
Before heading out for school

Seems like as I read
Things haven't changed so much
Folks wrangling for contracts and profit
After houses and cars and such

Had articles about those
achieving great degrees
Yet they have been getting those for years
Nothing for the better it seems
It's about who you know
And getting things
Collecting all the page fees

Decided to go to the grocery store
Had some things I had to get
Crowded as usual I said hello's
Faces filled with things
They would rather forget

I stood there for a moment
Watching the grocery line
This has gone on for ever
Just like the paper's headlines

Repeating all this history sublime
Seems like the thing to do
Endless lines that are meaningless
To fill my extra time

Degree in Political Science

Left Los Angles early
Will be traveling at 35,000 feet
Planes wings dipping down
I see the city scape
Dressing in its smoggy scene

Cars lined down the freeway
As far as you can see
They disappear into the city smog
To earn their daily means

How is it nothing changed
How is it that it seems worse
Perhaps it's that we are blinded
Pretending there is life on Earth

Is this the ways and means
As our satellite turns around
To harvest all the beautiful trees
Creating factories with colored scented smoke
Building hospitals to cure disease

How can we be so intelligent
To have blind eyes and hearts so numb
The rich bathe in profits and wealth
The poor bathe in poverty in the city slum

Get a degree in political science
Or maybe social welfare
No one seems to care enough
I will be at 35,000 feet real soon
As I pass through the smoggy fare

Guilded In Gold

Children wake in a dark cold hut
Meal cakes and dirty water
Food for the day is enough
Off to work
Little sisters and brothers
Little slaves
With all the others
Making bricks in the freezing cold
Hands and feet caked in mud
Breaking bricks from the molds
Children's work never done
Sunrise to sunset
In the fog dust and smoke
No time for play
There is a tally to make
1500 bricks a day

No toys no games
Making bricks
For the owners fame
Let's go on vacation
Let's go to the beach
Get a hotel room
Food fit for a king
Broken little lives
No song to sing
In a cold heartless world
Guilded in gold

In Due Time

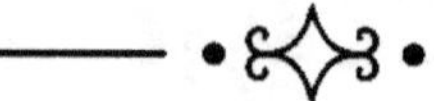

Can't be a martyr
Without dying
Can't be a hero
Without a cause
Can't have a heart
Without crying
Can't have a soul
Without love

The martyr born
To give his life
The hero
To win the day
The heart born
For laughter and pain
The soul
To search for a way

There is a life to die for
There is a price to pay
There is the night to bear up
There is a searching
For the day

Veil of Gold

Beyond the boundaries
Of earthly senses reign
A misty shroud
Hides a crystal plain
Stripped of the soul's
Earthbound hold
Another country
Appears untold
Speechless view
Fills the eyes
Boundless country
Boundless skies
Through the misty shroud
Majesty yet untold
Another country
Beyond the veil of gold

Caught Away

The demons shrugged their shoulders
At the frail human means
Their chains of deceit
Lead to enlightened dreams
They howl in glee
At the corruption of desires
The light of their darkness
Hide tunnels of despair
Opening paths to beauty and wealth
They entrap and twist with
Sadistic stealth
Eyes they feed with
Scales of esteem
A bright flash in the sky
Terrible screams on the earth
The Son of Man stands
At the door of Heaven's girth
A trumpet blows
Unnumbered angels dispatched
At command
God's remnant caught away
With a deafening sound
Holy, Holy, Holy Is The Lord

Rich And Poor

Woke up sweating in my bed
Tears filled my eyes
With grief and dread
Vision of cities burning
Smoke rising to the clouds
Cries of terror filled the air
No place to run
No place to hide
Escape is blocked on every side
News from nations groan and weep
At the sight of the destruction
God's judgement running deep
Rich and poor alike succumb
Cursing god for what is done
Their sin He judged
Upon His Son
He called He reached
He touched He healed
Their eyes blind with hate
Because of this
They would not come
He said in these last days
This would be done

Wiping my face with a cloth
Kneeling weeping
Crying
God forgive

God have mercy
My heart
My flesh
My soul
I am undone

Listening Eyes

A light haze comes
in the evening
The sun makes a veiled display
Shadows emerge from hiding
Nights eve slips quietly into place

Weather reports dense haze
Climate mongers claim the smog
Hunters claim giant bucks emerge
Politicians stalk a secret play

Ghettos sit in evening heat
Dreams made plans in vain deceit
The air is still and stale
But no one feels the pain

Hopeless days and nights contend
They end just as they begin
Traps laid for world control are made
Still and veiled in grave deceit

Only eyes upon heaven's throne
Have understanding of these days
They understand the working
Behind the veils and haze

No one listens
Eyes veiled from truth
Scrutiny of that secret day

Heavens Son comes into view
Angels and trumpets sound
The eastern sky
Filled with His blaze
He calls His own away

Lost Your Stars

Working day and night
Seems to never end
Got my pride
In the money
I spend

All my friends meet
At the Star Light Bar
We laugh and talk
And stretch the truth
Way too far

I said one more drink
And I have got to go
Got a new boss
Got to make a good show

Just bought a fast car
Like to push the speed
Blue lights flashing
I could not believe

Slapped on the cuffs
Spent the night behind bars
Called the boss first
He said don't worry son
Don't come back
You lost your stars

Central Intelligence

Young man graduates high school
A real special time in life
He was stoned as he could be
Grinning emptily into the camera
Bleary eyed for all to see
Raised most of his life in a stupor
Just wants another hit of crack
Learned his father's life skills
Living in a dark rotten shack
Walking in circles like a zombie
In confusion asking how a wheel turns
Jumps over a ditch of water
To set a pile of clothes to burn

There is a reason to exist
Ask him and he knows it all
How the sun stays in the sky
And the roundness of a ball

A very intelligent person
Lost all reasoning and sense
He learned it all from his father
Who always had a defense

Now in prison
Getting three square meals
He learned it all from his father
Living a life really real

He spent most of his time fishing
Cast himself sportsman of the day
A wasted life his reward
For a crack at life his fathers way

Man On The Curb

Well, it's Saturday morning
Time for groceries again
Friends coming to eat tonight
Good way for the week to end

Driving into the parking lot
Sits a man on the curb
With a cardboard sign asking for money
Must say when I see them
My heart is disturbed

The deed was done
Shopping finished
Looking forward to dinner
My excitement was growing

The man was still on the curb
As I looked we met eye to eye
My wife looked too
She started to cry

It was our own son
Left home years ago
We drove away
Picked up food for him

When we got back he was gone
We left a note saying
We love you please come home
We drove away

Walked out to get the paper next morning
Returning to the house
I saw the bag of food we brought to him
Sitting on the steps
I could not believe

It had a note on it
Still full of food
You could have loved me at home
All you have are words

Oh To Be A Dreamer

Oh to be a dreamer
Where nothing is real
Living in a shanty
On a palm tree covered beach
Crystal water sparkles
Roaring of the distant waves
Fish roasting on an open fire
Fresh bread toasts near the flames

Morning breeze blowing
Bright colored clothes dry in the sun
No questions to be answered
Nothing to prove achieve or get done
Children laugh playing in the sand and surf
You tell me is that not fun

Oh, to be a dreamer
Where nothing is real
Living in a shanty
On a dirty Chicago street
Overflowing colored trash cans
Plastic bottles shine
In an overgrown vacant lot
Anger and hateful words
Flow from an abandoned house
Smoke from an abandoned car
Stench fills the arid wind
Drug deal gone bad

Gunfire
A child's body in the street
Life goes on as usual
You smile undisturbed
Oh to be a dreamer
Where nothing is real
Nothing to really talk about
Go on dreaming forever

Stolen Dream

Life by design
Or skipped across the water
Like a rock
Impetuous to believe
I am of myself
A star hurdling across the universe
With no beginning or end
Spinning from one undefined place
To another
Why does it spin at all

An unmapped existence
A child in the slums
Suffers from cradle to grave
An emboldened tyrant
Planning
Errant corrupted ways
Life by design
Or a stolen masterpiece
From a majestic plan
The handy work of a masterful mind

Purchased for a Purpose

The streets are filled with fainting hearts
Eyes filled with vacant stares
The children's feet are filled with hate
There's trouble in the air

The search is on for something
Of what they're no quite sure
But hate, murder, and violence
We know is not the cure

The day is not over
Until another life is taken
The answer is in the
Word of God
When will our hearts be shaken

Prison cells are filled with lives
Purchased by Christ's own blood
What will it take to awaken your heart
It's in your own neighborhood

Jesus said if a man follow me
His own life he must deny
If our purpose is to survive
Another life will die

Jesus gave up His own life
Just for you and me
His mission must be taken up
Bringing souls into eternity

Perfection

Sitting on the porch
Reading Saturday morning papers
Fresh cup of coffee
Bold headlines read
Kidnappers make a stand
Twelve Children trapped
By mad men's minds
Four teens with weapons
Watched too many videos of crime
Had sharpened their skills
With video games
Played the parts out
With brilliant minds

Dark hearts laughing at the pain
Trained well on crime TV
To see a man die
It was all the same
Don't really care about the person's face
It's the power of control
At any expense in any place
To extinguish a life
Has been practiced to perfection
To die for this glory
To hell's resurrection
All hail Hollywood
To hell's resurrection

The Old Men's War

It was 1969
High School was done
Making plans
Married young
Got a letter in the mail
Uncle Sam needs your help
They sent me to train
To fight and kill in the jungle
At night
Went out on recon
Enemy secrets to find
We found them out
But our secret was laid bare
Escaping in the dark
Tracers lighting our way
Found ourselves out
On no man's land bay
Sun rising on the desperate scene
The LZ was surrounded
Out on the open beach
Called in fire on ourselves
From a battleship out of sight
Giant shells filled the air
Terror filled our eyes
The jungle destroyed
Friends in pieces on the ground
Two of us lay
On the bloody beach alone

These old men spent time
Making this plan
Sending young men
To bleed in foreign sand
Their patriotism so great
Locked in their planning rooms
My life is left haunted
By the faces left doomed
I'm alone at home
Years later on
The family is away
Can't take alone anymore
Must see my friends
The idea I was spared
Made no sense at all
Today was the day
I had to see them again
Left a note on the table
Said I was going away

The Damage Done

My window was open on a peaceful day
I heard the crack of a pistol
It wasn't far away
Picked up my phone
Got on my shoes
Hurried out to make
A personal survey

Got to the sidewalk's end
Heard sirens sounding nearby
A person kneeling near a body
Laying on the street course
Hurried closer to hear
Deep sobbing
Of a mother's deep remorse

A mother over her little boy
Covered in his blood
Holding him to her breast
His life had slipped away

Drug deal gone bad
Boyfriend would not get free
He stood there defending himself
Numb and heartless
With his smoking gun

She stands and beats him on his chest
Screaming it didn't have to be
He grabs her hands
He slaps her
Don't you know this is about me
The damage is done
The life is gone
The city bus stops to see
She screams dear god what will I do

The boyfriend slaps her again
Don't you get it
This is all about me

The Secret

Birth pangs cry out
Whether terror, pain or fear
Brought to one's end
The time draws near
Is it life
Is it death
Can loss be gain
Less become more
No escape
The struggle ensues
To become less and less
Empowered to live
Empowered to die
Deep in the inner man
The secret does lie
Possessing earth's bounds
Or heavens deep recess
What secret is it
Becoming more
Becoming less

Sixteen

Running out is an easy road
Can't face reality's ways
Hard to accept the truth
Of decisions that you made
Running out is an easy way
Can't think of anything else
Remember the past you left behind
Is that the future you hold
Running out is easy street
But is it really the best way
Better stick around
And make a change for the better
Leaving is a hard price to pay
Sixteen going on twenty-five
It's a hard row to plow
Too young to leave the child behind
Too young to leave just now

Can Anyone See

━━━ • ଽ◇ʒ • ━━━

Is anyone listening
Can anyone see
Seams of peace tearing apart
Children drinking confusion
As to nature's way
Is there no conscience
Can you only complain
Seams of peace destroyed
No one holy remains
No one seeks God's face
Prophets weep
No one chaste
Men are blind and cold
Children swept into the chase

Mans kingdoms are come
Mans will is done
His earth is scarred
Heavens doors closed
The watchmen are sleeping
Gates and walls broken down
Enemies laugh
At the religious toys
Violence consumes
Young men and boys
Is anyone listening
Can anyone see

The Color of Gold

Looking forward to the night
When sleep is the only friend
There is no need for food
Day has started as the end

Hunger has no preference
To the color of skin
Its desire runs deep
And shouts its demand

Lonely eyes look for comfort
A tin can rattles a single dime
The stomach cries out in hunger
It's all a matter of time

A damp cold room
Musty mattress on the floor
The single lamp
Hangs on a cord
And swings in the draft

Recognize the room
Know anyone there
Night time comes
Darkness is a friend
It hides the vacant stare
Whatever you have done
To the least of these

You have done it
Unto me
Won't you even take the time
To look
It's a nice Sunday morning
You took up your offerings
For the nice brick building
The decor is really bold

Padded pews
Stained glass windows
It really has looks to kill

It all really has
Just the right tone
The color of your heart
A pale shallow color of cold

What Will Be

Eyes that see
But never perceive
Ears that hear
But never receive
Hearts that beat
But never have life
Feet that run
But never arrive
Pointless labor
An endless sea
To always become
But will never be

Sunday Best

Wolves dressed up
In their Sunday best
Real nice offerings
Their staff attests

Designing programs
To draw them in offerings grow
So does the sin

Got emotions going
Choir got lights and smoke
Pretty singers singing
Preacher dances for the folks

Great philosophy
Makes them feel real nice
Some are getting chilly bumps
Some fall to add some spice

Jesus weeps kneeling on the floor
Warned that this would come
He writes Ichabod
Above the door

He leaves weeping
They would not come

Pretender

Make believe woman
Make believe man
Playing in a dangerous game
You act like something
You're really not
It's really so very plain

You talk to all the right people
You say all the right words
But deep down inside
You know you're living a lie
Man have you got the nerve

It's interesting to watch you
In action
You know you can really
Play the part
But when it comes to making
The real test
You know you're not very smart

So, fooling you're not
Not even yourself
It's a game you can never win
To know you is like seeing
A chameleon
In this case
The pretender is you

Market Place

Do you trust in things that are lasting
Or things that grow old in the sun
Life's not an emotional web
Always spinning what's already spun
It's not clothes, shoes or money
It's not fortune or fame in the world
It's not the armies or power of people
Marching their cause with flags unfurled
It's not knowing all the right people
It's not a name you drop in the hat
So what will you sell your life to
What price do you offer for that
Don't sell yourself on the market
It will always be too cheap
The price paid for your soul
It was very extremely deep
Heaven's doors are always open
Make its entrance way your goal
Watch out for your price
The world is attractive and nice
It's a fast pace
In the market place for souls

Thought for a Minute

Thought for a minute
Things might change
Thought for a minute
A way might come
Thought for a minute
The web would tear
Thought for a minute
But the minute was gone

Thought for a minute
There might be peace
Thought for a minute
For a change of heart
Thought for a minute
Things might change
Thought for a minute
But the minute was gone

Do you think fear will rule
That peace would find way
To escape the grip of hate
No love was found
No place of return
No place of retreat

Thought for a minute
Things might change
But the minute was gone

Answers Please

I walked to my window and
Pulled the curtain back
Looking down at the street
A cloudy misting windy day
Blowing the tree leaves
Enough to send some paper
Recklessly along the walk below
A young man caught my attention
His head bowed down
Shoulders hunched
Seeming mindless staring
As he leaned against
The brick wall across the street
As he tossed his cigarette
He moved crossing the street
In a purposeless pace
Not even looking for the traffic
Had all hope gone
Had he no home
Did he roam about alone
Was he spending another day
In a mindless haze
How was this to end
Were the news headlines his fortune
Another body found in an alley
No identification
How are the chains of
Misfortune to be cut

How many passed him daily
On some busy crowded street
Is he not significant
But to who though
Is destiny this dark
Is purpose so illusive
How is this to end
Grief grips my heart and soul
Tears in my eyes
A mournful prayer I sighed
Dear God in heaven
Please send him an answer
God whispered
Into my grieving heart
You are my answer

On My Own

Came home late again
Breath smelling of whisky and gin
Just stopped to get one drink
Time got away it's 4am

Pulled up in the drive
Her car was gone
The door was open
There was no one home

A note on the table
Me and the kids are gone
We won't be back
You can do this alone

She told me time again
That she had had enough
Raising kids alone
I'm putting you on the shelf

Looked in the bedrooms
She had packed and gone
My heart sank in my chest
I'm no one on my own

I fell down to my knees
I wept myself to sleep
Woke up sun was rising
My heart dark for the misdeed

I cried to the Lord
Please help me out
I pushed her over the line
The phone rang in a strange way

She said
I love you
I will be home late
I forgive you
God said go back home

I fell back on my knees
My heart broken in pieces
I give my life to you god
Please help and save my soul

Help me be the man
That I need to be
I am really weak
As you can see

Make me strong
To make this right
I've been so wrong
Change me today

Unknown Way

Time is not a friend
To the masses
Free or slave
It judges men's souls
With an unsuspected tone
Played out before a master
No one speaks His name
Time is not a friend
To the soul
Free or slave
Nothing can satisfy him
Deep longings of his soul
One does not know why
An unseen master
With an unspeakable name
Hides the secret
For an unknown day

Voice of conscience
Lends itself to this secret
It ties or releases the soul
To the master in an unknown way
How careful time is traveled
Narrow paths to ends unknown
Care ensued with plans and dreams
The master comes on an unknown day
Caution with time
On this unknown way

Mr. Lonely

Lonely man, lonely night
Lonely heart, lonely fight
Got in my car
Try to make a new start
Down the road
Was no friend in sight

Not going back home
I had lost it all
Many miles in pride
I was on a free fall
The road was dark
There was a cheap hotel
Had nothing left
I felt close to hell

In the lonely room
With a lonely heart
Got on my knees
To make a new start
Talked to God for an hour or so
He said go back home
Make it right you know
Asked for forgiveness
He touched my heart
Went back home
Made a humble start

I Still See Your Face

Went to bed in a stupor
Did not know if I would awake
I was shaken almost out of my bed
Jesus walked into my place

Saved out of my delirium
I shook myself awake
He looked with such compassion
Stepped back to heavens place

I see His face everywhere
The children in the street
Look at me from every nation
Every land across the sea

Had to leave my country
Their hearts have grown so numb
I followed His glory far away
They were waiting for me to come

Beautiful children in Africa
Needing to be loved
Can't escape their faces
Their laughter in a simple place
Beautiful mothers leaving Venezuela
Chased like rats into the night
No food no bed
No breast to keep the baby fed

Beautiful people in Mexico
Demons at every corner shop
Keeping lies in oppression
Casting them out of their souls

There is no place I can go
That I do not see His face
His compassion possesses
My very soul
He is walking everywhere
He waits in the very next place

You Don't Know Me

You don't know me
You just recognize my face
You hear my voice
And know it's mine
But you don't know me
And that's just fine

You don't know me
You just see me around
You don't know where I've been
The faces and lives
In places of renown

You don't know me
I've walked the streets
In distant lands
Seen the children's faces
In the streets where
To live or die is easy

You don't know me
I loved mothers, fathers, strangers
That will never know relief
Want and hunger
Are their plans
A broken heart
To meet their demands

You don't know me
Perhaps it's better that way
My heart is in another place
Another country
And that's okay

Traveling On

I'm walking down this lonesome road
I'm holding on to your hand
I'm going on a path unknow
I'm holding onto your hand

Can't no one walk this road for me
It's set into my destiny
Can't know the way
It's by faith I see
I'm holding onto your hand

I've not been down this road before
It's an unfamiliar way
I've not been around this way before
I'm holding onto your hand

There's a valley behind and a mountain before
I'm holding onto your hand
I'm traveling on
I know with you I can
I'm holding onto your hand

Can't no one walk this road for me
It's set into my destiny
Can't know the way
It's by faith I see
I'm holding onto your hand

It's a long and narrow road you see
But it's all a part of destiny
There is no other way for me
Holding on to my Masters hand

Waiting For Sunrise

Sitting on a corner
Waiting for the sun to rise
Darkness has hidden the way
Waiting for the Daystar
To come and stay

I've been sitting in this darkness
So hard to find the path I took
No one to guide
The right way seems to hide
Waiting for the Daystar
To come and stay

You would think someone could see me
The loneliness deep inside
Too busy looking for themselves
Looking for the Daystar to light my way

Oh that my steps were sure
Oh that my path was set
I feel miles from the nearest hope

I'm waiting patiently
Haste cannot be wise
Waiting for the daylight
Waiting for the Daystar
To come and stay

Waiting for the sunrise
To come my way

Not Just Luck

I set my feet on solid ground
Not on shifting sand
I hold on to the Word of God
On His promises I stand

Man's promises are but a step away
They fall as they begin
I hold on to the Word of God
By faith I stand within

The world is tossing to and fro
There is no future there
If only in this world you hope
Your future is cold and bare

So I walk by faith and not by sight
As I hold His promise dear
It's by His strength I carry on
In this I have no fear

It's by His word from day to day
I know it's not by luck
I've tried it on my own before
It's a good way to stay stuck

Set your feet upon the Rock
And there you make a stand
There is no hope in this old world
Its ways are sinking sand

Please Take A Seat

Woke up this morning
Hands on my head
Sat upright
Almost fell out of bed

Talk of strikes and layoffs
Barely making ends meet
Wife's been crying at night
Kids are losing sleep

Daughters got cancer
Have no insurance for that
Medicine gets bought
That's about that

Wife got a job
At the corner store
Too much pressure
Don't consider us as poor

Got to work early
They called us in to meet
I've got bad news to tell you
Will you all take a seat

They called us in one by one
Grown men came out in tears
What is this they have done
They kept lying amid all our fears

Pink slip in hand
I walked to my locker
It was my very last day
It was a complete and total shocker

Not knowing what to do
I cried out dear God
Can't do this without you
Driving home I got a call
From a long lost friend

He said I was just thinking of you
If you were still at your old job
I had a position come up
Like you to come see me today

Started a job the very next day
I told my wife she said no way
I said yes even making more money
God's hand moved
How glorious honey

Filling His House

The time is getting near
The house is being shaken
The old is passing away
The house is being awaken
The Lord's touch is drawing near
His hand is reaching out
The threshing floor is filling u
He's coming there is no doubt

The choices are becoming clearer
The dark and light becoming far apart
The house is held in godly fear
The time is growing very short
The time is getting nearer
His voice is getting clearer
His promise is upon us
Open hearts will hear it

He's filling
His house
It's in clear view
He's filling me
He's filling you
He's filling this house

About the Author

Author Thomas S. Doland served in the military as an infantryman from 1969 to 1975. During this stint, he learned something of the art of war. He was married in 1969 and had two daughters: one in 1974 and one in 1976. He had a deep experience with God in 1976, which captured his life for missionary service to Africa, India, South America, and Mexico. His love for humanity grew and continues to be his reason to live and breathe. He is directing and financing a school for child slaves in a brickyard in Pakistan, keeping him focused on presenting his writings to challenge and provoke thought outside of common life. Love embraces him and he hopes for love to embrace you to seek and fulfill your purpose